# State Fair

by Julie Murray

Dash!
**LEVELED READERS**
An Imprint of Abdo Zoom • abdobooks.com

3

## Dash!
### LEVELED READERS

**Level 1 – Beginning**
Short and simple sentences with familiar words or patterns for children who are beginning to understand how letters and sounds go together.

**Level 2 – Emerging**
Longer words and sentences with more complex language patterns for readers who are practicing common words and letter sounds.

**Level 3 – Transitional**
More developed language and vocabulary for readers who are becoming more independent.

THIS BOOK CONTAINS
RECYCLED MATERIALS

**abdobooks.com**

Published by Abdo Zoom, a division of ABDO, PO Box 398166, Minneapolis, Minnesota 55439.
Copyright © 2020 by Abdo Consulting Group, Inc. International copyrights reserved in all countries.
No part of this book may be reproduced in any form without written permission from the publisher.
Dash!™ is a trademark and logo of Abdo Zoom.

Printed in the United States of America, North Mankato, Minnesota.
052019
092019

Photo Credits: Alamy, Getty Images, iStock, Shutterstock, © Sergey Galyonkin p20 / CC BY-SA 2.0
Production Contributors: Kenny Abdo, Jennie Forsberg, Grace Hansen, John Hansen
Design Contributors: Dorothy Toth, Neil Klinepier

**Library of Congress Control Number: 2018963306**

**Publisher's Cataloging in Publication Data**

Names: Murray, Julie, author.
Title: State fair / by Julie Murray.
Description: Minneapolis, Minnesota : Abdo Zoom, 2020 | Series: Fantastic fairs |
    Includes online resources and index.
Identifiers: ISBN 9781532127250 (lib. bdg.) | ISBN 9781532128233 (ebook) |
    ISBN 9781532128721 (Read-to-me ebook)
Subjects: LCSH: State fairs--Juvenile literature. | Agricultural fairs--Juvenile
    literature. | Fairs--Juvenile literature.
Classification: DDC 394.6--dc23

# Table of Contents

State Fair . . . . . . . . . . . . . . . . . . 4

The Midway . . . . . . . . . . . . . . . 8

Food and Entertainment . . . . 12

More Facts . . . . . . . . . . . . . . 22

Glossary . . . . . . . . . . . . . . . . . 23

Index . . . . . . . . . . . . . . . . . . . 24

Online Resources . . . . . . . . . . 24

State Fair

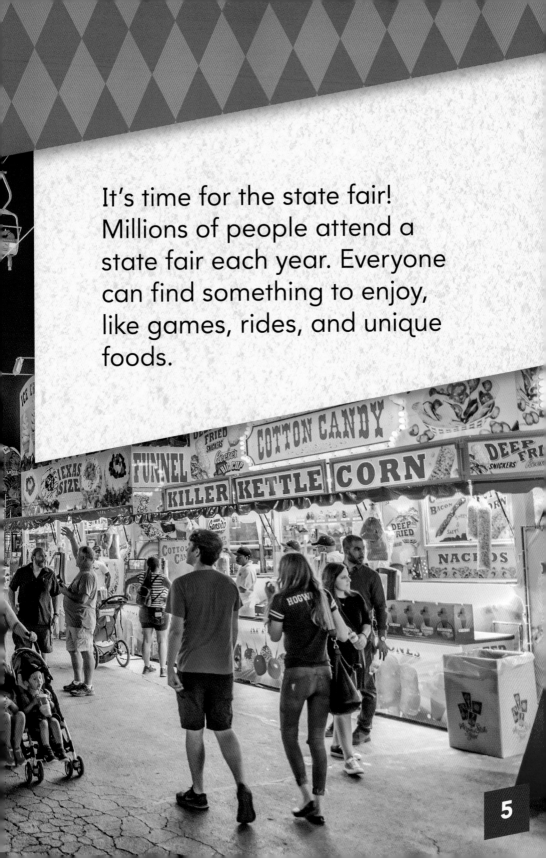

It's time for the state fair! Millions of people attend a state fair each year. Everyone can find something to enjoy, like games, rides, and unique foods.

Almost every state has a state fair. Pennsylvania is a state that does not. Most state fairs last 10 to 12 days. The Texas State Fair runs for 24 days!

# The Midway

A state fair is not complete without the **midway**. This is where rides, games, and much more can be found. Giant slides, Tilt-a-Whirls, and bumper cars are all found at the midway.

The state fair is a great place to test your skills and luck at games. The horse racing game and ring toss are a few favorites. Winners can walk away with large stuffed animals or fun toys.

# Food and Entertainment

Be sure to come hungry to the state fair! Food on a stick is a fairgoer favorite. At the Iowa State Fair, there are more than 70 different foods served on a stick!

The fair also has exciting contests.
People make jams, cookies, pies
and grow **produce** to be judged.
Winners take home a blue ribbon!

15

There are also animals at the
state fair. Visitors can see live
births and newborn animals
at the Birth Center.

**4-H** is a big part of the fair too. Kids can win prizes for the **livestock** they have helped raise.

17

Marching bands often perform at state fairs. Grandstands have live shows each night. The Minnesota State Fair grandstand has seating for 17,000 people!

19

Demolition derbies, monster trucks, and sandcastle building are all part of state fairs too. There is something for the whole family to enjoy at the state fair!

# More Facts

- The Great New York State Fair is more than 175 years old. It is the oldest state fair in the US. It started in 1841 in Syracuse.

- The Alaska State Fair is older than the state. It began in 1936. Alaska became an official state 23 years later in 1959.

- The Minnesota State Fair has the largest daily attendance. It averages around 200,000 visitors each day!

# Glossary

**4-H** – a US-based network of youth organizations whose mission is to engage youth to help them reach their fullest potential. Programs having to do with agriculture, science, engineering, technology, and more are available.

**livestock** – cows, horses, sheep or other animals raised or kept on a farm or ranch.

**midway** – the area or strip where food stands, shows, and games are found at fairs.

**produce** – things made or grown in order to be sold, especially fresh fruit and vegetables.

# Index

4-H 17

animals 16, 17

attendance 5

Birth Center 16

contests 14

duration 7

entertainment 18, 20

food 5, 12, 14

games 5, 8, 10

grandstand 18

Minnesota State Fair 18

music 18

prizes 10, 14

rides 5, 8

Texas State Fair 7

# Online Resources

**Booklinks**
**NONFICTION NETWORK**
FREE! ONLINE NONFICTION RESOURCES

To learn more about state fairs, please visit **abdobooklinks.com** or scan this QR code. These links are routinely monitored and updated to provide the most current information available.